PLAYS FOR PERFORMANCE

*A series designed for
contemporary production and study
Edited by
Nicholas Rudall and Bernard Sahlins*

MARIVAUX

The Dispute

In a New Translation by
Gideon Lester

With a Foreword by
Anne Bogart

Ivan R. Dee
CHICAGO

Library of Congress Cataloging-in-Publication Data:
Marivaux, Pierre Carlet de Chamblain de, 1688–1763.
    [Dispute. English]
    The dispute / Marivaux ; in a new translation by Gideon Lester.
       p. cm. — (Plays for performance)
    "This translation was first performed on February 1, 2003, at the American Repertory Theatre, Cambridge, Massachusetts, in a production directed by Anne Bogart in association with the American Repertory Theatre"—P. 9.
    ISBN 1-56663-555-1 (alk. paper)
    I. Lester, Gideon. II. Title. III. Series.

PQ2003.D55E5 2004   2003064646

FOREWORD
by Anne Bogart

Marivaux's plays are magnificent dense dramatic gems of incredible charm and power. His prismatic wordplay, the inherently theatrical landscapes, and the ever-surprising sophistication and emotional depth found within these seemingly simple tales of lovers scheming to conquer one another make the plays a magnet for actors and directors everywhere.

I chose *The Dispute* because to me it is the most mysterious and attractive of all Marivaux's plays. The story is as simple as the story of Adam and Eve and also as complex and meaningful.

But how to begin? How to approach this elegant puzzle? One afternoon, while sitting outside my farmhouse in upstate New York drinking coffee and watching the pigeons mate on top of my barn, the world of the play was suddenly revealed to me. I saw it directly in the pigeons' elaborate mating dances. We, humans and nonhumans alike, are caught in an everlasting waltz of sexual interplay. I decided to investigate this irrational dance and our biological proclivity to disorient and conquer one another as we try to find a mate. I knew instinctively how useful this would be in staging *The Dispute.*

That summer Gideon Lester came to visit me at my farmhouse so that we might discuss the translation and the production. He arrived on the hottest day of the year, and we placed lawn chairs precariously on the spot that offered the most promise of a breeze. We opened the text in French and began to read the first scene. But we did not get very far that day, not due to the heat but because the tricky translation issues immediately loomed large and seemed to me almost insurmountable. Relieved that Gideon would be the one who would have to wrestle with these linguistic problems, I moved on to discuss birds and mating rituals with him.

Gideon's translation of *The Dispute* is, to me, miraculous. He has managed to find a lightness and wit that is both true to the original and great to speak out loud. He arrived at rehearsal with a finished translation but remained open and receptive to the actors' reactions and thoughts as we moved ever so slowly through the treacherous waters of the play. Together we discovered how deceptive the simple chain of scenes and events are and how they mask a rather profound reification of the world itself. Did I use the word "tricky" already? "Tricky" would be the most descriptive word I can find to describe the feat of performing this tightrope-walk of a play.

The text in French is refractive, mathematical, and awesome. Gideon found an accurate reflection in English, and thanks to his elegant feat of translation we are able to enter precisely into the unique world of Marivaux.

INTRODUCTION
by Gideon Lester

When I began work on this version of *The Dispute*, I assumed the translation would take a matter of weeks. The play is short—the French text fills a scant thirty pages—and at first glance the narrative seems slight. I was wrong. Every word Marivaux wrote is part of an intricate game, a series of interlocking puzzles that dramatizes the creation of language itself. Each of the play's four young lovers must literally learn a new vocabulary with each fresh encounter. When Églé first emerges into her captors' garden, she has no words to denote the world she discovers there. Streams, mirrors, men—her new life brings with it a whole new lexicon. When Azor first meets Églé, he has no language to describe what he sees or the emotion he feels. "The pleasure of seeing you has robbed me of words," he tells her. Within a matter of pages, these linguistic neophytes are engaged in a battle of words that rivals Coward or Wilde in its sophistication. The birth of their self-knowledge—as humans, as individual men and women, as members of society—by necessity brings with it the birth of a language. Rendering that process into English proved to be a game of its own.

Marivaux's verbal mastery is such that the choice of each word, each phrase, is freighted with meaning. Many of his constructions are simply untranslatable, because they rely on tricks of gender, mood, or tense that have no equivalent in English. On first seeing Azor, Églé notes *"La personne rit, on dirait qu'elle m'admire."* She refers to Azor as *"elle"*—she—because the French *personne* is feminine; but a French listener would also enjoy the solipsism of a woman who has never met a man and therefore assumes that all humans are known as "she."

Other cruxes require more creative strategies, carrying us still further from Marivaux's text. As Adine terminates her showdown with Églé she awards herself one of the greatest exit lines of all time, *"Mon mérite est son aversion."* Elegant and perfectly balanced, it's also untranslatable into English, a language notoriously hostile to abstract nouns. "My merit is her aversion"? Meaningless. To translate the phrase more accurately you would need to expand it—"What's worthy in me is what she loathes"—which destroys the concision, and therefore the point, of her put-down. My solution was to create a different rhetorical flourish, an internal rhyme that conveys Adine's attempt to rescue her self-possession: "My splendors offend her."

Translating is a solitary business until you enter rehearsal; thereafter it can be a pleasure or a pain. Working with Anne Bogart and the SITI Company on *The Dispute* remains one of the greatest pleasures I've had in the theatre. The physical rigor and virtuosity of this legendary ensemble is matched by their intelligence and love of language. Anne and her cast responded to a few stylistic hints in this elusive text and from them created a production of indescribable elegance and vigor, which managed to switch genre in every scene while maintaining a profound integrity of style and substance. No one who saw *The*

6

Dispute in Cambridge, Massachusetts, will forget Frank Raiter's magnificent pomposity as the Prince, or the curl of Lynn Cohen's lip as she mouthed, *"libertinage de sentiment"* (a line of Marivaux's that surely cannot be spoken in English). Ellen Lauren's Églé began as a fledgling sparrow fallen from her nest, grew to an arch seductress, and ended as the heroine of a neoclassical tragedy. The central encounter between Églé and Adine (Kelly Maurer channeling Ethyl Merman) somehow combined the drawing-room, manners of Gwendolyn and Cecily with a low-down vaudeville catfight, as the two women thumped each other with ever-expanding white exercise balls. Azor bonded with Mesrin in—where else?—a locker room, while Carise and Mesrou frolicked through the copper passages of Neil Patel's shimmering set, which somehow managed to evoke a labyrinth, a bird's nest, the hall of mirrors at Versailles, a Richard Serra sculpture, an amphitheatre, and a broken heart. Every aspect of the production was deeply silly and highly serious, which seems to me entirely in the spirit of Marivaux.

Since Patrice Chéreau's celebrated production in 1973—the play's first revival since its premiere in 1744—*The Dispute* has been in almost constant performance in France, where the extent of Marivaux's innovation has now been fully recognized. Following Chéreau's lead, many directors now add a prologue to the play, often dramatizing the debate at the Prince's court that precedes Marivaux's first scene. Anne and her company also devised a prologue, initially composed of fragments from other texts by Marivaux, which framed *The Dispute* as an episode in an endless war between tribes of men and women.

Halfway through rehearsals Anne discarded the language of the prologue and replaced it with a silent sequence, part dance, part mime, which grew out of the SITI Company's famous technique of physical composition known as "the Viewpoints." Each member of the ensemble entered, one by one, dressed in James Schuette's monochromatic gowns that combined the fashions of eighteenth-century Paris and contemporary grunge. They preened in front of an invisible mirror that ran the length of the proscenium, then entered a dark world of watching and waiting where they mocked, cruised, and fought each other in an ever-shifting choreography that exploded as a wild tango. The Prince and Hermiane silently watched the pageant, as if observing younger incarnations of themselves at play. Amused, disturbed, and finally furious, Hermiane interrupted this stylized battle of the sexes by launching into her dialogue with the Prince, and so Marivaux's play began.

The wordless prologue grew from a discovery that Anne and the company made early in rehearsals; despite the garrulousness of Marivaux's characters, their silence is as dramatically important as their speech. The text may be short, but productions of *The Dispute* regularly run close to two hours. Each character undergoes more profound psychological transformations than in many plays three times the length, and *The Dispute* can well support a slow presentation. Églé's first brief encounter with Azor lasted over five minutes in the American Repertory Theatre production, as each learned how the other moved, walked, talked, felt, and smelled. The game of the play lies in watching each human experience

8

discovered anew, and that takes time. It's worth re-membering that Marivaux wrote most of his plays for a company of Italian *commedia dell'arte* actors who spoke little French and relied heavily on physical gesture to communicate. His dialogue, for all its wit and panache, is only the tip of the iceberg.

Finally, a note on the text. At times Marivaux punctuated his dialogue in a somewhat expressionistic way, eliding sentences to suggest haste or anger. Wherever possible I've preserved his structures in English—"Oh now, easy, she's not your girl, she's mine, both these hands are mine, you've got nothing." "Come here Mesrin, what are you doing over there, are you crazy?" Actors may find such constructions useful or choose to ignore them. Likewise Marivaux's frequent exclamations—"Ah!" "Eh!" "Oh!"—which the SITI actors often used to suggest that animal grunts and cries lay only just beneath the surface of all that linguistic sophistication.

CHARACTERS

HERMIANE

THE PRINCE

MESROU

CARISE

ÉGLÉ

AZOR

ADINE

MESRIN

MESLIS

DINA

THE PRINCE'S ATTENDANTS

The play takes place in the countryside.

This translation was first performed on February 1, 2003, at the American Repertory Theatre, Cambridge, Massachusetts, in a production directed by Anne Bogart, in association with the SITI Company.

The Dispute

Scene 1

HERMIANE: Where are we going, Seigneur? This is the most savage, solitary place in the world, with no sign of the show you promised me.

PRINCE: *(laughing)* Everything's prepared.

HERMIANE: I understand none of it. What kind of house is this you bid me enter, this peculiar construction? Why is it encircled by so many vast walls? Where are you leading me?

PRINCE: To a strange spectacle indeed. You remember the question that rattled us last night? You maintained, alone against all my court, that it was not *your* sex but *mine* that pioneered betrayal, that invented unfaithfulness in love.

HERMIANE: Yes, Seigneur, I maintain it still. Whoever it was, that first betrayer was brazen enough to blush at nothing. Women's nature was ever shy and modest, and is so still, despite the world and its corruption. How could women have first committed these sins of the heart that require such audacity, such effrontery, such *libertinage de sentiment*? It's beyond belief.

PRINCE: Eh! Of course, Hermiane. I think it no more plausible than you. You don't have to argue with me. I'm on your side, against the rest of the world. You know that.

HERMIANE: Yes, but only out of gallantry. I have watched you carefully.

PRINCE: Gallantry? It is true that I love you, and I suppose my great urge to please you might have convinced me you were right, but if it did I swear I never felt it. A man's heart is worth nothing—you're welcome to it. No question, it's more liable than a woman's to be fickle and faithless. My heart alone is safe, and only because it finds itself in love with you.

HERMIANE: Your speech smacks of irony.

PRINCE: Then I shall soon be punished for it. I'll show you how to undo me if I don't truly think as you.

HERMIANE: What do you mean?

PRINCE: Yes, we'll consult Nature herself. Only she can decide the question definitively, and I have no doubt she will find in your favor.

HERMIANE: Explain yourself. I don't understand a word.

PRINCE: For us really to know whether the first infidelity, the first betrayal, was committed by a man, as you claim, and so do I, we'd have to have witnessed the creation of the world and of society.

HERMIANE: Of course. But we didn't.

PRINCE: But we will. Oh yes, the men and the women of that time, the world and its first lovers, will soon appear before our eyes exactly as they were, or as they must have been, in essence if not in every detail. You will see the same landscape of the soul, hearts just as pure as those very first hearts, or even purer. *(to Carise and Mesrou)* Carise, you may go, and you, Mesrou, and when it's time for us to withdraw, give the signal we agreed on. *(to his attendants)* Leave us, if you please.

Scene 2

HERMIANE: You've piqued my curiosity, I confess.

PRINCE: Here are the facts. Eighteen or nineteen years ago the very same dispute arose at my father's court, where it raged long and hard. My father was something of a philosopher, and although he was not of your mind, he resolved to settle the matter with an experiment that would leave no room for doubt. Four newborn babies, two of your sex, two of mine, were brought into the forest, where he'd had this house built especially, where each of them would live in isolation, and where each still remains in a world they have never left, beyond which they have never seen. They know no one but Mesrou and his sister, who raised them and who still care for them, and who were chosen for their color so that their protégés might be the more amazed when they finally saw other people. Now for the first time they will be granted the freedom to leave their enclosures and meet. They've been taught our language, and we can observe their interactions as if we were watching the dawn of the world. Love will be born as if for the first time. Let's see what happens next. *(the sound of trumpets)* But come, we must withdraw. This gallery runs the length of the building, and from it we'll be able to see and hear whatever transpires between them. Let's go.

Scene 3

CARISE: Come, Églé, follow me. Here's a new land you've never seen before. It's quite safe, you can look around.

ÉGLÉ: What's this I see? Oh, brave new world!

CARISE: It's the same old world. You just never knew how huge it was.

ÉGLÉ: All this country! All these buildings! I feel like I'm nothing in such a big space! I'm so happy! I'm so frightened! *(she sees and stops beside a stream)* What's this? Water, flowing on the ground? I've never seen anything like it in the world I come from.

CARISE: Quite right. That's what's called a stream.

ÉGLÉ: *(looking)* Ah! Carise, come here! Look, there's something living in the stream! It's made like a person, and she seems as amazed at me as I am at her!

CARISE: *(laughing)* Eh! No, that's you you're seeing! All streams do that.

ÉGLÉ: What! That's me, that's my face?

CARISE: Of course.

ÉGLÉ: But you know that's really quite lovely. Oh, what a charming thing I am! Too bad I didn't know sooner.

CARISE: It's true. You are pretty.

ÉGLÉ: Pretty? I'm gorgeous! What a magnificent discovery! *(she looks at herself again)* The stream does all my faces, and I love all of them. You and Mesrou must have adored looking at me. I shall spend the rest of my life contemplating me, and soon I'll even fall in love with myself.

CARISE: Take a walk around. I'll leave you and go back to your house. There's something I need to do there.

ÉGLÉ: Go, go, I won't get bored, not with the stream.

Scene 4

(Églé is alone for a moment. Azor appears opposite her.)

ÉGLÉ: *(continues, considering her face)* I'll never grow tired of myself. *(and then, noticing Azor, in terror)* What's that? Is she a person, like me? Don't move! *(Azor holds out his hands admiringly and smiles; Églé continues)* The person is laughing, as if she admires me. *(Azor takes a step)* Stop! Though I do like the way she looks at me. . . . Do you know how to speak?

AZOR: The pleasure of seeing you has robbed me of words.

ÉGLÉ: *(happily)* The person can hear me, she answers me, and so nicely!

AZOR: You are ravishing!

ÉGLÉ: Oh good.

AZOR: You are enchanting!

ÉGLÉ: I like you too.

AZOR: Then why do you forbid me to come nearer?

ÉGLÉ: I don't really forbid you any more.

AZOR: Then I'll step closer.

ÉGLÉ: I'd like that. *(Azor comes closer)* Wait . . . I'm so nervous. . . .

AZOR: I obey, because I'm yours.

ÉGLÉ: She obeys! Then come over here so you can be mine closer. *(Azor comes)* Look at her! Isn't she lovely? No really, you're just as pretty as me.

AZOR: I'm dying of joy to be beside you, I give myself to you, I don't know what I'm feeling, I don't know how to say it.

ÉGLÉ: Me too.

AZOR: I'm happy, I'm flustered.

ÉGLÉ: I'm sighing.

AZOR: No matter how close I get, I can't see enough of you.

ÉGLÉ: I was thinking the same thing, but there's no way we could see more of each other. We're already here.

AZOR: My heart desires your hands.

ÉGLÉ: Take them—my heart gives them to you. Are you happier?

AZOR: Yes, but no calmer.

ÉGLÉ: Nor me. We're completely the same!

AZOR: Oh—we're so different! All that I am is not worth your eyes. They're so tender.

ÉGLÉ: Yours are so alive!

AZOR: You are so darling, so delicate!

ÉGLÉ: Yes, but I assure you it becomes you not to be so delicate as I am. I wouldn't want you any other way—you're a different kind of perfect. I embrace my perfection. Safeguard yours for me.

AZOR: I will never change it. I will keep it always.

ÉGLÉ: Oh yes! Tell me, where were you all that time before I met you?

AZOR: In a world of my own that I'll never go back to since you are not there, and I long always to hold your hands. Neither I nor my mouth shall ever abandon your hands.

ÉGLÉ: And my hands shall never abandon your mouth. But I hear a noise! Those people are from my world. You mustn't frighten them—hide behind the trees. I'll call you.

AZOR: Yes . . . but I won't be able to see you.

ÉGLÉ: No—you have only to look in this flowing water. My face is there. You'll see.

Scene 5

ÉGLÉ: *(sighing)* Ah! Already am I weary of its absence!

CARISE: Églé, you seem troubled. What's the matter?

MESROU: Even her eyes look softer than usual.

ÉGLÉ: I have big news. You think there are only three of us but I have to break it to you—we're four. I happen to have acquired something that just a second ago was holding my hand.

CARISE: Something's been holding your hand, Églé? Why didn't you yell for us to rescue you?

ÉGLÉ: Rescue me from what? From the pleasure I felt? I was very glad it held my hand. I gave it permission to hold it. It kissed it very much, and I only have to call it back and it'll kiss it again because I want it to, and it wants to too.

MESROU: I know what it is. I think I even glimpsed it as it snuck away. The thing is called a man. It's Azor. We know him.

ÉGLÉ: Azor? Pretty name! Dear Azor! Dear man! He'll be back.

CARISE: I'm not at all surprised that he loves you and you love him. You were made for each other.

ÉGLÉ: Right. We worked that out for ourselves. *(she calls him)* Azor, my Azor, come quickly, oh man!

Scene 6

AZOR: Eh! It's Carise and Mesrou. They're my friends.

ÉGLÉ: *(cheerfully)* They said you were made just for me, and me just for you. That's why we love each other so much. I'm your Églé, you're my Azor.

MESROU: He's the man and she's the woman.

AZOR: My Églé, my joy, my delight, my woman!

ÉGLÉ: Here, hold my hand. It's compensation for having to hide. *(to Mesrou and Carise)* See, this is what he was doing before. Should I have yelled for you to rescue me?

CARISE: My children, I've already told you. You were fated to attract each other.

ÉGLÉ: *(holding his hand)* It's wonderfully simple.

CARISE: But there's one thing you must do if you're to love each other always.

ÉGLÉ: Yes, I know, we must always be together.

CARISE: On the contrary. You must sometimes deprive yourselves of the pleasure of seeing each other.

ÉGLÉ: *(astonished)* What?

AZOR: *(astonished)* Huh?

CARISE: Yes, because if you don't, that pleasure will decrease and you'll grow indifferent.

ÉGLÉ: Indifferent! Indifferent, to my Azor? Ha ha ha! That's very funny!

AZOR: *(laughing)* What does she know?

MESROU: Don't laugh—she's giving you excellent advice. It's only by doing as she says and separating from time to time that Carise and I still love each other.

ÉGLÉ: Oh yes, I can well believe that, it's probably true for you two because you're so black. You must have fled in fear the first time you saw each other.

AZOR: Probably it was all you could do to put up with yourselves.

ÉGLÉ: And you'd soon be sick of each other if you didn't spend time apart, since there's nothing lovely about the way you look. I mean, I like you, but when I don't see you I don't miss you. Why don't I have to have you around? Because I don't find you attractive, whereas we are attractive to each other, Azor and me. He's so handsome, I'm so beautiful, so gorgeous, that every time we see each other we're stunned.

AZOR: *(taking Églé's hand)* Here's Églé's hand, do you see, just her hand, but I'm in agony when I'm not holding it, and when I am holding it I die if I can't kiss it, and when I've kissed I die anyway.

ÉGLÉ: The man's right. I agree with everything he says. You talk of our pleasure, but you have no idea what it is. We don't understand it, and we feel it. It's infinite.

MESROU: We're only suggesting you separate for two or three hours a day.

ÉGLÉ: Not for one minute.

MESROU: Pity.

ÉGLÉ: You're annoying me, Mesrou. Are you saying that looking at each other will make us ugly? Will we stop being attractive?

CARISE: No, but you'll stop feeling it.

ÉGLÉ: Eh! What's going to stop us feeling attractive if we still are?

AZOR: Églé will always be Églé.

ÉGLÉ: Azor always Azor.

MESROU: Of course, but who knows what could happen? Suppose I were to become as handsome as Azor, or Carise as beautiful as Églé?

ÉGLÉ: How would that affect us?

CARISE: You might grow sick of each other and be tempted to break up and love us.

ÉGLÉ: What do you mean, "tempted"? Why would we leave what we love? Is that logical? Azor and I love each other, and that's that. Be as beautiful as you like, how does that affect us? It's your business. Ours is complete.

AZOR: They'll never understand. You have to be us to know what it's like.

MESROU: As you say.

AZOR: Love is my life.

ÉGLÉ: Do you hear that? It's his life. How could he leave me? He has to live, and so do I.

AZOR: Yes, my life. How could anyone be so lovely, with such lovely eyes, and lovely lips, such lovely everything?

ÉGLÉ: I love it when he admires me!

MESROU: It's true he adores you.

AZOR: Oh, well said! I adore her! Mesrou understands me. I adore you.

ÉGLÉ: *(sighing)* Adore me then, but give me time to breathe! Ah!

CARISE: It's so sweet even I find it touching. But there's only one way you can preserve it—you must believe us. And if you're smart enough to decide, here Églé, give this to Azor. It'll help him bear your absence.

ÉGLÉ: *(taking a picture that Carise gives her)* What is it? I recognize this—it's me! It's me again, and much better than in the stream. It's all my beauty, it's me! What joy to find myself everywhere! Look, Azor, look how charming I am!

AZOR: Ah! It's Églé, it's my dear woman, there she is! Although the real thing is even lovelier. *(he kisses the picture)*

MESROU: It does look like her.

AZOR: Yes, and it makes me want her. *(he kisses it again)*

ÉGLÉ: There's just one problem. When he kisses it, my picture gets everything.

AZOR: *(taking her hand, which he kisses)* We can solve that problem.

ÉGLÉ: Ah! But I want one to play with too.

MESROU: You have to choose—his picture or yours.

ÉGLÉ: I'll keep them both.

MESROU: Oh no, please decide. I'd like one of them.

ÉGLÉ: Oh well, in that case I suppose you should keep Azor's, since I already carry his portrait in my heart, so give me mine and then I'll have both.

CARISE: Here it is, in a different form. We call it a mirror. You just press here to open it. Goodbye, we'll

28

come and find you soon. But I beg you, think over the separations.

Scene 7

ÉGLÉ: *(attempting to open the box)* Let's see. I can't open it. You try, Azor. Here's where she said you press it.

AZOR: *(opens it and looks at himself)* There! But it's only me. I think that's my face—a stream over there showed it to me.

ÉGLÉ: Ah! Ah! Let me see! Eh! You're completely wrong, man, it's me, more than ever. Honestly, it's your Églé, it's really her. Come and look.

AZOR: Eh! Yes, it's you. But wait, it's both of us—half you and half me. I'd like it better if it was just you. I'm preventing myself seeing all of you.

ÉGLÉ: Ah! I'm quite pleased to see a little of you too. You don't spoil the view. Come closer. You hold it.

AZOR: Our faces are going to touch. Look, they're touching. See how happy mine is? Oh, what happiness!

ÉGLÉ: I can feel your touch, and I like it very much.

AZOR: What if our mouths came closer? *(he takes a kiss)*

ÉGLÉ: *(turning)* Oh! You've ruined it—now I can only see me! This mirror is a marvelous invention.

AZOR: *(taking the picture)* So is the picture. *(he kisses it)*

ÉGLÉ: You know, Carise and Mesrou are decent people.

AZOR: They only want what's best for us. I was going to talk to you about them, and the advice they gave us.

ÉGLÉ: You mean the separations? I was wondering about that too.

AZOR: Églé, their prediction frightened me. I'm not in the least worried on my account, but don't you start getting bored with me or I'll be desperate.

ÉGLÉ: It's yourself you should worry about. Don't you ever stop loving me. Even though I'm gorgeous, your fear is frightening me too.

AZOR: Beloved! You've got nothing to worry about. . . . What are you thinking?

ÉGLÉ: Okay, okay, all things considered, I've decided. Let's make ourselves miserable and separate for two hours. I love your heart and your adoring me even more than your being here, though I like that too.

AZOR: What! Separate?

ÉGLÉ: Ah! If you don't do as I say, I may suddenly not want to any more.

AZOR: Alas! I don't have the strength.

ÉGLÉ: Too bad. Neither do I.

AZOR: *(crying)* Goodbye, Églé, since we must.

ÉGLÉ: You're crying? Oh dear, then stay—if there's really no danger.

AZOR: What if there is?

ÉGLÉ: Then go.

AZOR: I'm leaving.

Scene 8

ÉGLÉ: Ah, he's gone, I'm alone, I can't hear his voice, there's only the mirror. *(she looks into it)* I was wrong to send my man away. Carise and Mesrou don't know what they're talking about. *(examining herself)* If only I'd looked at myself properly, Azor would never have gone. You could love this sight forever, you don't need separations. . . . Ah well. I'll sit by the stream again. Now I have two mirrors.

31

Scene 9

ÉGLÉ: But what do I see? It's another person again!

ADINE: Ah! Ah! What's that new thing over there?

(she comes closer)

ÉGLÉ: It's examining me carefully but not at all admiringly. That's not an Azor. *(she looks at herself in her mirror)* It's even less an Églé, but I think it's comparing us.

ADINE: I don't know what to make of that face. I don't know what it's missing. It's a little insipid.

ÉGLÉ: Whatever it is, I don't like the look of it.

ADINE: Does it speak? Let's see. Are you human?

ÉGLÉ: Yes, I assure you, very human.

ADINE: Is that so! Yet you have nothing to say to me?

ÉGLÉ: No. Generally I am spoken to. People address me.

ADINE: But do you not find me charming?

ÉGLÉ: You? I'm the charmer.

ADINE: What, are you not pleased to see me?

ÉGLÉ: Alas! Neither pleased nor perturbed. Should I be?

ADINE: Well, here's a mystery! You see me, I let myself be seen, and you feel nothing? You were surely distracted. Consider me more closely. There. How do you find me?

ÉGLÉ: Why so much talk of you? Were we discussing you? I tell you it's me people look at, it's me they tell how I look, that's how it's done, yet you think I should consider you, even though I am here!

ADINE: Of course—it's the responsibility of the loveliest person to wait until someone notices her and is dazzled.

ÉGLÉ: So, be dazzled!

ADINE: You don't listen, do you? I said it's the responsibility of the loveliest person to wait.

ÉGLÉ: And I said she's waiting.

ADINE: But if she's not me, where is she? I have won the admiration of the only three other people in the world.

ÉGLÉ: I'm not acquainted with your people, but I know three whom I captivate and who regard me as wondrous.

ADINE: And I know that I am so lovely, so lovely, that I tell you I'm charmed every time I see myself.

ÉGLÉ: You tell me? I tell you whenever I catch a glimpse of myself, I'm enchanted.

ADINE: Enchanted! It's true you're passable, maybe even quite pretty—you see, I'm being fair, I'm not like you.

ÉGLÉ: *(aside)* I'd like to take her fairness and slap her in the face.

ADINE: But for you to believe there's any room for dispute—well you must be joking. It's plain to see.

ÉGLÉ: What's plain to see is you.

ADINE: I get it. You're jealous, and that prevents you finding me beautiful.

ÉGLÉ: It's your face prevents me.

ADINE: My face! Oh! But you don't upset me, for I've seen my face. Go ask the waters of the flowing stream how it is, ask Mesrin, who adores me.

ÉGLÉ: The waters of the stream that make you look a fool would assure me there's nothing lovelier than I, in fact they have already. I've no idea what a Mesrin is, but he wouldn't look at you if he'd ever seen me. I have an Azor who's worth much more, an Azor whom I love, who is almost as attractive as I, and who says I am his life. You are no one's life. And what's more, I have a mirror that confirms beyond a doubt everything the stream and my Azor tell me. How's that?

34

ADINE: *(laughing)* A mirror! You have a mirror too! And what's it good for? Admiring yourself? Ha ha ha!

ÉGLÉ: Ha ha ha! I knew I'd loathe her.

ADINE: *(laughing)* Look, here's a better one. Come learn to know yourself and to shut up.

(Carise appears in the distance)

ÉGLÉ: *(laughing)* Take a glance in this one. You'll discover your mediocrity and the modesty that befits you in my presence.

ADINE: Pray get you gone. Since you refuse to take pleasure in the sight of me, I have no use for you, and I'm not talking to you any more.

(they don't look at each other)

ÉGLÉ: I don't know you're there.

(they walk in opposite directions)

ADINE: *(aside)* She's a lunatic.

ÉGLÉ: *(aside)* She's hallucinating. What kind of world bred her?

Scene 10

CARISE: Now what are you two doing so far apart and not talking?

ADINE: *(laughing)* This is a new person I bumped into. My beauty has driven her to despair.

ÉGLÉ: What do you make of this faded thing, this absurd specimen who strives to amaze me, who asks how I feel when I see her, who expects me to rejoice at her sight, who says to me, "Eh! Stare at me, won't you? Eh! What do you think of me?" and who maintains she's as beautiful as I!

ADINE: I didn't say that, I said more beautiful, as she could see if she looked in the mirror.

ÉGLÉ: *(showing her mirror)* Let her look in this one, if she dare.

ADINE: I only ask her to take a peek in mine, which is more accurate.

CARISE: Gently now, don't lose your tempers. You should be glad to have met. Let's join forces! You should be friends and add your pleasure at seeing each other to your happiness in being both adored, Églé by dear Azor whom she cherishes, Adine by dear Mesrin whom she loves; so come on, make up.

36

ÉGLÉ: Only if she abandons her wearisome delusions of beauty.

ADINE: Wait—I know how to make her see sense. I just have to take her Azor from her. I don't want him, but anything for a little peace.

ÉGLÉ: *(enraged)* Where is this stupid Mesrin of hers? Good luck to her if I find him. So long, I'm moving on, I've had all I can stand.

ADINE: Ha ha ha! My splendors offend her.

ÉGLÉ: Ha ha ha! What a silly face!

Scene 11

CARISE: Come on, let her say what she likes.

ADINE: Of course, you're right. I pity her.

CARISE: Let's go. It's time for your music lesson. I won't teach you if you're late.

ADINE: I'm coming, but I see Mesrin. I must have a word with him.

CARISE: You just left him!

ADINE: Won't be a moment.

Scene 12

ADINE: *(calling)* Mesrin!

MESRIN: *(rushing over)* What? It's you, it's my Adine, she's back! How happy I am! How impatient I was!

ADINE: Hey now, don't get too happy, I'm not back, I'm going, I just happened to be here.

MESRIN: Then you'll just have to happen to be here with me.

ADINE: Listen, listen, I've got something to tell you.

CARISE: Keep it short, I have things to do.

ADINE: I know. *(to Mesrin)* I am beautiful, aren't I?

MESRIN: Beautiful! Oh, you're beautiful!

ADINE: He doesn't hesitate, he says what he sees.

MESRIN: You're a goddess! You're Beauty herself!

ADINE: Yes, that's what I think. Nevertheless, you, Carise, and I—we're all wrong. I'm ugly.

MESRIN: My Adine?

ADINE: Really. When I left you I found a new person who's from another world and who, far from being astonished by me, being transported by me like

38

you are and like she should have been, wanted *me* instead to be charmed by *her*, and when I refused, accused me of being ugly.

MESRIN: You'll make me lose my temper!

ADINE: She said that if you saw her, you'd leave me.

CARISE: Only because she was angry.

MESRIN: Is she really human?

ADINE: She says she is, and she looks like one, more or less.

CARISE: Of course she is.

ADINE: She'll surely be back, and I absolutely want you to loathe her when you see her. I want you to find her terrifying.

MESRIN: She sounds horrible.

ADINE: Her name . . . wait a moment . . . her name is . . .

CARISE: Églé.

ADINE: Yes, it's an Églé. And this is what she looks like: an angry, scowling face that isn't black like Carise's or white like mine—it's a color you can't really describe.

MESRIN: It's not nice?

ADINE: Oh no, not at all, it's nondescript. She has eyes—how do I put this?—eyes that do nothing for her, they just look, that's all; a mouth neither large nor small with which she talks; a straightish figure, very straightish, that would actually be more or less like mine if she were nicely put together; hands that flit about; long, skinny fingers, I think; with a rude, sour voice—oh, you'll recognize her.

MESRIN: I can just see her. You leave her to me, I'll send her packing to her other world as soon as I've really embarrassed her.

ADINE: Really humiliated her, really upset her.

MESRIN: And really mocked her. Oh, don't you worry, and give me this hand.

ADINE: Here, take it. I keep it only for you.

(Mesrin kisses her hand)

CARISE: *(taking her hand)* All set, come on, let's go.

ADINE: When he's done kissing my hand.

CARISE: Leave it, Mesrin, I'm late.

ADINE: Farewell, my only love, I shan't be long. Dream of revenge!

MESRIN: Farewell, my only delight. I am enraged!

Scene 13

MESRIN: *(the first words alone, repeating the description)* Color not black nor white, a straightish figure, a mouth that talks . . . where would I find such a thing? *(seeing Azor)* But I see someone, it's a person like me—or could that be Églé? No, she doesn't seem at all deformed.

AZOR: *(looking him over)* And don't you look like me?

MESRIN: I was thinking the same thing!

AZOR: So are you a man?

MESRIN: That's what they tell me.

AZOR: That's what they tell me too.

MESRIN: They tell you—you mean you know people?

AZOR: Oh yes, I know all three of them.

MESRIN: Me too! Where are you from?

AZOR: The world.

MESRIN: My world?

AZOR: Oh, I don't know. There are so many now.

MESRIN: Who cares? I like how you look. Give me your hand. We should fall in love.

41

AZOR: Okay. You make me feel better. I like looking at you, though you're not very pretty.

MESRIN: Nor are you. I wouldn't give a damn about you if you weren't such a guy.

AZOR: That's right, that's why I like you, you're a good buddy—and I'm a good buddy. Who cares about faces?

MESRIN: Yeah, man—I'm just happy, that's why I'm looking at you. By the way, do you eat food?

AZOR: Every day.

MESRIN: Awesome! Me too! So let's eat together—it'll be fun, it'll help keep us in a good mood. Come on, it's nearly time. We'll laugh, we'll jump, right? I'm already jumping.

(he jumps)

AZOR: *(also jumping)* Yeah, me too, so there'll be two of us—or maybe four if I tell my girl about this—and she's got a face—you should see it! Ha! Ha! Her face is worth more than both ours put together.

MESRIN: Oh, I believe you, buddy, because you're nothing, and I'm nothing, compared to this other face I know, and she'll hang out with us too, and she drives me wild, she's got these hands, they're so sweet, and she lets me kiss them so much!

42

AZOR: Hands, buddy? My girl has hands that are like divine, and I get to stroke them whenever I want. I'm expecting them now.

MESRIN: Super! I've just left mine, and now I'll have to leave you too. There's a little business I got to take care of. So wait here till I come back with my Adine. Let's jump together one more time to celebrate our new friendship. *(they jump together, laughing)* Ha ha ha!

Scene 14

ÉGLÉ: *(coming nearer)* What's this that's giving you so much fun?

MESRIN: *(seeing her)* Oh! What a beautiful thing is looking at us!

AZOR: It's my girl, it's Églé!

MESRIN: *(aside)* That's Églé of the angry face?

AZOR: Ah! I'm so happy!

ÉGLÉ: *(coming nearer)* Is this another new friend who suddenly appeared?

AZOR: Yes, this is my buddy, he's called "Man," and he comes from a world close to here.

43

MESRIN: Oh, this world is so fun!

ÉGLÉ: More fun than yours?

MESRIN: Uh huh.

ÉGLÉ: Well then, Man, you'll just have to stay.

AZOR: That's what we were saying, since he's so cool and happy. I like him—not like I like my gorgeous Églé whom I love—I don't really care about him much, I just want to have him around so I can talk about you, your mouth, your eyes, your hands, that I've been pining for.

(he kisses one of her hands)

MESRIN: *(taking her other hand)* I'll just take the other one.

(He kisses that hand. Églé laughs and doesn't say a word.)

AZOR: *(taking that hand from him)* Oh now, easy, she's not your girl, she's mine, both these hands are mine, you've got nothing.

ÉGLÉ: He didn't mean any harm, but while we're on the subject you can go now, Azor, you know how vital separation is, and ours hasn't been long enough.

AZOR: What! It's been I don't know how many hours since I last saw you!

ÉGLÉ: You're wrong, it hasn't been long enough in fact. I do know how to tell time, and when I've decided a thing I mean to stick by it.

AZOR: But then you'll be on your own.

ÉGLÉ: Ah well, I'll survive.

MESRIN: Don't upset her, buddy.

AZOR: I think you're mad at me.

ÉGLÉ: Why are you being so stubborn? Didn't they say there was nothing so dangerous for us as seeing each other?

AZOR: Maybe it's not true.

ÉGLÉ: I doubt they were lying.

(Carise appears in the distance, listening)

AZOR: All right, I'll go if it makes you happy, but I'll be back soon. Hey buddy, didn't you have a little business to take care of? Come with me, help me pass the time.

MESRIN: Yes but. . . .

ÉGLÉ: *(smiling)* What?

MESRIN: I've been walking so long.

ÉGLÉ: He needs a rest.

MESRIN: I'll stop the lovely lady getting bored.

ÉGLÉ: Oh yes, he will.

AZOR: Didn't she say she'd rather be alone? Otherwise I would unbore her better than you. Let's go!

ÉGLÉ: *(aside and annoyed)* Let's go!

Scene 15

CARISE: *(approaching Églé and watching her as she daydreams)* What are you thinking?

ÉGLÉ: I'm thinking I'm not in a good mood.

CARISE: Are you upset?

ÉGLÉ: Not upset—heavyhearted.

CARISE: Why so?

ÉGLÉ: You told us that when you fall in love, you can never tell what might happen?

CARISE: That's right.

ÉGLÉ: Well then, I can't tell what might happen.

CARISE: What's wrong with that?

ÉGLÉ: I seem to be mad at myself, mad at Azor, and I don't know what it means.

46

CARISE: Why mad at yourself?

ÉGLÉ: I'd planned to love Azor forever, and now I'm afraid I won't.

CARISE: Is that a possibility?

ÉGLÉ: Yes, and I'm furious with Azor because his behavior's to blame.

CARISE: It sounds like you're picking a fight with him.

ÉGLÉ: If that's all you can say, then soon I'll get mad at you too.

CARISE: You certainly are cranky. What's Azor done to you?

ÉGLÉ: What's he done? We agree to separate, he goes, he comes back immediately, he wants to be here all the time—in the end what you told him will happen will happen.

CARISE: What—you'll stop loving him?

ÉGLÉ: Of course. If the pleasure at seeing each other goes when it's had too often, is that my fault?

CARISE: You told us you were certain that could never be.

ÉGLÉ: Don't split hairs. How could I tell? I was certain because I didn't know.

CARISE: Églé, it can't be his eagerness to see you that makes you dislike him—you haven't known him long enough.

ÉGLÉ: Quite long enough—we've already had three conversations, and evidently the length of our encounters is counterproductive.

CARISE: You still haven't said how he's hurt you.

ÉGLÉ: In many ways. I don't know how many. First, he annoys me. My hands are mine, I think, they belong to me, and he forbids them to be kissed!

CARISE: And who wants to kiss them?

ÉGLÉ: A friend he picked up out of the blue—he's called Man.

CARISE: And he's attractive?

ÉGLÉ: Oh, stunning, nicer than Azor, he even offered to stay here and keep me company, and Azor, the lunatic, wouldn't grant him either my hand or my company, he growled at him and rudely carried him off without so much as asking me what I wanted. Ha! Ha! Am I suddenly no longer the mistress of my life? Can he suddenly not trust me? Is he suddenly afraid that someone might love me?

CARISE: No, he's worried you might find his friend attractive.

ÉGLÉ: Well, all he has to do is attract me more. If it's a question of being loved, I'm delighted to be, and that's that. And if instead of one friend he had one hundred, I'd want them all to love me. I live for love! He wants my beauty to be his alone, but I protest it must be for the world!

CARISE: Listen, your distaste for Azor has nothing to do with any of that. Right now you just happen to love his friend more than him.

ÉGLÉ: You think so? Maybe you're right.

CARISE: Ha! And tell me, aren't you just a touch ashamed of your infidelity?

ÉGLÉ: I suppose I am a little embarrassed by my accident. I'm still ignorant of such matters.

CARISE: You are no such thing! You promised many times to love him faithfully.

ÉGLÉ: Listen, when I promised, he was all there was. He should have stayed all there was. I didn't know he'd get a friend.

CARISE: Come on, that's a lousy excuse, you said so yourself.

ÉGLÉ: You're right, it's not good, but here's a great one—the friend's much better than Azor.

CARISE: You're still kidding yourself. He's not better, he has the advantage of being new.

ÉGLÉ: Quite an advantage, or doesn't "new" count? Doesn't "different" count? It's certainly attractive, and something Azor lacks.

CARISE: Not to mention that the newcomer will fall in love with you.

ÉGLÉ: Of course he'll fall in love with me—I hope so, and that's attractive too.

CARISE: Whereas Azor isn't going to fall in love with you.

ÉGLÉ: Eh? No, he loves me already.

CARISE: Strange grounds for a change of heart! I bet it doesn't make you happy.

ÉGLÉ: Nothing makes me happy. On one hand the change hurts, on the other it gives me pleasure. I can't stop feeling either of them, they're both real. To which do I owe most? Must I hurt myself? Must I please myself? Advise me, I challenge you.

CARISE: Consult your heart—you'll find it loathes your infidelity.

ÉGLÉ: Why aren't you listening? My heart loathes it, my heart loves it, it says yes, it says no, it's in two minds, and I can only choose the most convenient.

CARISE: Do you know what you should do? Escape from Azor's friend. Let's go, come on, you'll be rid of the struggle.

ÉGLÉ: *(seeing Mesrin approach)* Yes, but escape is too late—look, the struggle's back, here comes the friend.

CARISE: So what? Take heart! Be strong! Don't look at him!

MESROU: *(from a distance, trying to keep hold of Mesrin, who escapes)* He's escaping me, he wants to be unfaithful, don't let him get any closer!

CARISE: *(to Mesrin)* Stop! I forbid you to move!

MESRIN: Why?

CARISE: Because I say so. Mesrou and I must keep some authority over you—we're your masters.

MESRIN: *(rebelling)* My masters? You're not my masters.

CARISE: All right, I won't order you, I'll beg you, and the fair Églé adds her prayers to mine.

ÉGLÉ: Nothing of the kind. I never beg.

CARISE: *(to Églé, aside)* Let's go inside. You're still not sure he loves you.

ÉGLÉ: Oh, but I don't hope he doesn't—we only have to ask him. What do you desire, handsome friend?

MESRIN: To see you, to watch you, to admire you, to call you my life.

ÉGLÉ: You see, he's speaking of his life. Do you love me?

MESRIN: Beyond hope.

ÉGLÉ: What did I tell you?

MESRIN: Do you love me too?

ÉGLÉ: I'd rather not if I can help it, because of Azor. He's counting on me.

MESROU: Mesrin, do as Églé. Don't be unfaithful.

ÉGLÉ: Mesrin! The man's called Mesrin!

MESRIN: Eh, yes.

ÉGLÉ: Adine's friend?

MESRIN: I was, but I now have no need of her portrait.

ÉGLÉ: *(taking it)* Her friend and her portrait—this deal's getting better and better. Ha ha! Carise—he has so many selling points, how can I resist? Come, Mesrin, that I may love you.

MESRIN: How sweet this hand that now is mine!

ÉGLÉ: How dear this friend, and now he's mine!

MESROU: But why are you leaving Adine? Did she somehow hurt you?

MESRIN: No, this lovely face requests it.

ÉGLÉ: He has eyes, that's all.

MESRIN: I know I'm unfaithful, but I can't help it.

ÉGLÉ: Yes—I'm forcing him. We're forcing each other.

CARISE: Azor and Adine will be in despair.

MESRIN: Too bad.

ÉGLÉ: What can you do?

CARISE: If you like, I could end their suffering by making them fall in love.

MESRIN: Oh yes, do!

ÉGLÉ: Oh no, don't. I'll be glad if Azor mourns me—my beauty warrants it. And it's not so bad if Adine suffers a little. That'll teach her to overrate herself.

Scene 17

MESROU: Here comes Azor.

MESRIN: I'm embarrassed—my buddy's in for a surprise.

CARISE: From his face, I'd say he's guessed the wrong you've done him.

ÉGLÉ: Yes, he is sad—ah! And with good cause. *(Azor steps forward, ashamed; Églé continues)* Are you upset, Azor?

AZOR: Yes, Églé.

ÉGLÉ: Really?

AZOR: Very.

ÉGLÉ: He does seem upset. Ah! How did you know I love Mesrin?

AZOR: *(astonished)* What?

MESRIN: Yes, buddy.

AZOR: Églé loves you, she doesn't care for me?

ÉGLÉ: It's true.

AZOR: *(delighted)* Eh! That's great! Carry on—I don't care for you either. Wait a moment—I'll be back.

ÉGLÉ: Now *you* wait a moment. What are you trying to say? You don't love me any more? What's that supposed to mean?

AZOR: *(going)* You'll see.

Scene 18

MESRIN: Were you calling him back? What's that about? What do you want with him now that you love me?

ÉGLÉ: Oh, leave me alone. I'll love you more if I get him back. I just don't want to lose anything.

CARISE AND MESROU: *(laughing)* Ha! ha! ha! ha!

ÉGLÉ: Glad you find it funny.

Scene *19*

ADINE: Good day, fair Églé! If ever you wish to see yourself, address yourself to me. I have your portrait. I was given it.

ÉGLÉ: *(throwing her hers)* Here, take yours back, it's not worth the trouble of keeping it.

ADINE: What, Mesrin, my portrait? How does she have it?

MESRIN: I gave it to her.

ÉGLÉ: Now then. Azor, come here. I wish to speak to you.

MESRIN: Speak to him? What about me?

ADINE: Come here Mesrin, what are you doing over there, are you crazy?

Scene 20

HERMIANE: *(entering briskly)* No, Seigneur, let me go. I've seen more than I can bear. I find this Adine and this Églé intolerable—Fate seems to have chosen for us the two very most hateful members of my sex.

ÉGLÉ: Who are all these people who rush in and snarl? Run for your lives!

(they all try to escape)

CARISE: Stay where you are, don't be scared, these newcomers are friends. Let's not frighten them but hear what they have to say.

MESLIS: *(stopping in the middle of the theatre)* Oh, my sweet Dina, look at these people!

DINA: Yes, but they have nothing to do with us.

MESLIS: You're right, not one of them looks like you. Ah, Carise and Mesrou! All these people—are they men or women?

CARISE: As many women as men. Here's one kind, there's the other. Take a look at the women, Meslis. If you find one you like more than Dina, she shall be yours.

56

ÉGLÉ: I want to be his friend.

MESLIS: Better not to want what you can't have.

CARISE: Choose another.

MESLIS: Thank you—it's not that I dislike them, I just don't like them. There's only one Dina in the world.

DINA: *(throwing her arm on his)* Very well said.

CARISE: Now you, Dina. Take a look.

DINA: *(taking him by the arm)* I've seen all I need to. Let's keep going.

HERMIANE: Sweet child! I'll take care of her.

PRINCE: And I of Meslis.

DINA: We're quite all right on our own.

PRINCE: You'll never be parted. Go, Carise, have them set aside, and see the others dealt with according to my orders. *(and to Hermiane)* Neither sex has reason to reproach the other, Madame. Vice and virtue, both own their share.

HERMIANE: I beg you, admit some distinction. The treachery of your sex is vile, you change your hearts without reason, without even searching for an excuse.

57

PRINCE: I admit your sex's strategy is more hypocriti-
cal and therefore more civilized—you make more
fuss about conscience than we do.

HERMIANE: Trust me, we have no grounds for laugh-
ter. Let's go.